Books Susan Ioannou

Spare Words
Motherpoems
Familiar Faces/Private Grief

CLARITY
BETWEEN
CLOUDS

Poems of Midlife

SUSAN IOANNOU

to Mary and Bill — in appreciation for your support and love of poems,
Susan Ioannou

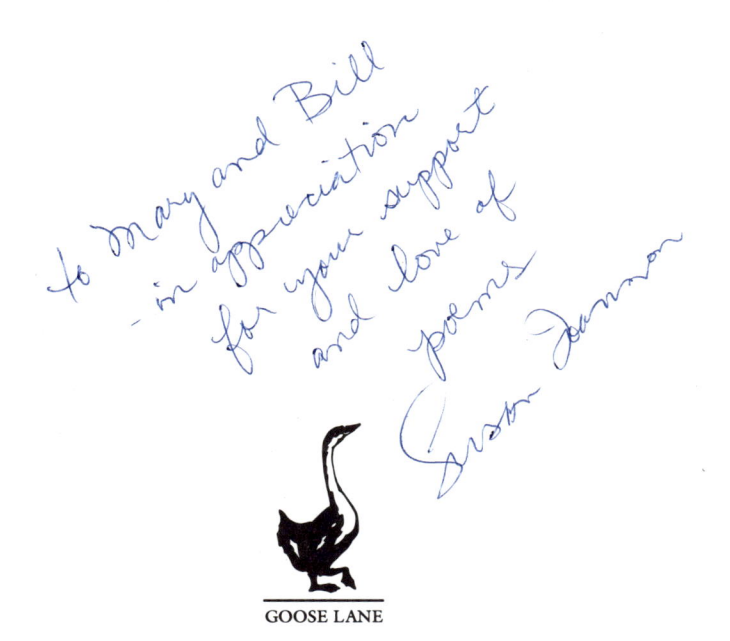

GOOSE LANE

© Susan Ioannou, 1991.
All rights reserved. No part of this publication may be reproduced, stored in a retrieval system, or transmitted, in any form or by any means, electronic, mechanical, photocopying, recording, or otherwise, without the prior written permission of the publisher.
Some of these poems have appeared in *And Other Travels, The Antigonish Review, Arts Scarborough Newsletter, The Blotter, Celebrating Canadian Women, Cross-Canada Writers' Quarterly, Contemporary Verse 2, Dandelion, Daybreak, Green's Magazine, HMS Press Poetry Broadsheet, The New Quarterly, Northward Journal, Poetry Canada, Poet's Gallery, Potato Eyes, Prairie Journal of Canadian Literature, Prism International, Quarry, Songs From The North, Souldust And Pearls, White Wall Review.*
Published by Goose Lane Editions with the assistance of the Canada Council, 1991.

Cover art: "From the North Shore, Lake Superior" by Lawren S. Harris, 1929, oil on canvas, 122 cm x 152 cm, collection of the London Regional Art and Historical Museums.
Book design by Julie Scriver.
Printed in Canada by The Tribune Press.

Canadian Cataloguing in Publication Data
Ioannou, Susan 1944-
Clarity between clouds

Poems.
ISBN 0-86492-111-X

I. Title.

PS8567.0263C52 1991   C811'.54   C91-097662-7
PR9199.3.I62C52 1991

Goose Lane Editions
361 Queen Street
Fredericton, New Brunswick
Canada E3B 1B1

For Larry, Polly and Stefan

CONTENTS

PART I
RIMMING THE DARK

Crystal   11
Last Photographs   12
Pink & Indigo   16
Before The Portrait Of Lucrezia Panciatichi   19
Across The Piazza   20
Perdika   21
My Prussian Past Holds No Comfort   22
Sea Deep, At St. Kitts   24
Persimmon   25
Sudden Absence   26
Dusk, Highway Seventeen   27
Fast   Slow   Fast   28
A Double Hook   29
Boardwalk, Early Morning   30

PART II
THE BLACK SPECK

Perfect Canvas   33
Domestic Artistry   34
If Age   35
Kathleen Marshall   36
Convalescent   37
Eileen And Jean   38
In Your Light   40
Waves   43
Old Black Cat   44
Small Comforts   46

Elegy   50
Balance Sheet Dream   52

PART III
DAWN SNOW

Dawn Snow   55
Baptism   56
Haiku   57
Poem In February   58
Treasure Hunt   60
McDiarmid Watches The Children Fishing   61
Mothering Days   62
Runaways   64
The Little Dancers   66
Dusk, Edwards Gardens   67
After The Cub Meeting   68
Bath/Beddy   69
At The Ontario Science Centre   70
Solstice   72
First Snow   73
The Wheel   74

PART I
RIMMING THE DARK

CRYSTAL

Like a crystal spinning in light,
too many choices
blind the heart.

Words are no longer inscribed in stone,
but flash beyond paper, undulant sound,
too many, too fast.
Uncertainties whirl us around.
What can it mean
to be wise?

Must we turn to the rock
as it slips under water,
reach with evergreens
after a rushing sky?
Will the land's solid curve remind
how gold freezes to white
yet remains the same?

We tingle from *Yes, No,* to *Why*
without realizing
how dizzy we've grown,
without even knowing
if forward or back
leads home.

LAST PHOTOGRAPHS
For Merla McMurray

I

Across rhododendrons, hollyhocks, roses,
summer fades from your garden.
Tall sons have gone.

The dark one, with delicate wrists,
the older one, blond, big-boned . . .
letters from Europe to open as light falls.

Little boys echo, then vanish,
evening's last showers of gold.

II

And you, in beige lace, Irish linen,
surface smooth as an unstrung pearl,
watch night clouds slide down.

Leaning within the darkened bay window,
slowly you twist the rings round your finger.
Where does the future begin?

England?
Provence?
Rome?

> The wealthy Umbrian farmer
> raising his glass at the marble-topped table
> sweeps the air with wide hands:
>
> "All my young days
> around the whole world I have travel.
> Here is the best. I stay."

An acre of earth
— or inside our heads —
where do we wander, describe what is real?

> Twenty years motoring weekly to King's College,
>   Cambridge,
> painting seventeen hundred precise watercolours'
> intricate revelations of cornice and spire

to the fat American guest at her Tate retrospective
    "I grow roses,"
    Lady Brockington sums up her life.

Remember the luminescence of Turner country,
mists burning pastels into simple canvas:
"Romantic Abstraction," the art critic claims.

You know better, have touched their soft fire.
Dreams are the same:
what is there, to be known.

III

But first the tangled plants must be taken down,
rooms emptied of complications,
the armoire sold for a comfortable wicker chair.

Kindred spirits murmuring dust from their frames
stop you, walking down a long hall.
You study their secret faces, and wonder

> what train whistles into the evening,
> when is the channel crossing,
> before the shutter's last click?

PINK & INDIGO
For Merla McMurray

I

Behind pink neon
glowing against night's indigo,
we sit within the wide café window,
and over chilled lettuce leaves and pâté
watch the world pass.

Watercolours on off-white walls
lie quiet: orderly rows of Italian roofs
tiled in pink, blue pastels.
Their existence is framed, without change
except, imperceptibly at first,
to fade when exposed to light.

We love the darkness for that reason.
Imagination flushes our colours bright
as the curved pink chair, where a wizened lady
puffs defiance under her broad pink brim.
Smoke uncurls between pink nails,
drifts pink rings down jacket and skirt,
dissolves between pink hose and shoes.
She turns, and her crinkled smile puffs us pink too.

Outside, a streetcar climbs the slope,
sliding with purpose, who knows where.
Electric-lit faces, framed like stills,
glide as the movie draws them along.
— And where are we headed, behind pink neon
gazing into the night?

II

To be. To feel the sun
redden our evening faces,
board upon board blurring under our feet,
as daylight dwindled, we walked away the beach
— and back, for no reason, against a rising wind.

Here where the rhythms of wave and breathing
intersect the sun's slanted warmth,
we stand at the beginning: water and sand.
In this light, edges show sharp
the vastness, yet simplicity of living:

> we grow older
> gardens wither
> step by step
> children, husbands
> leave us
> to ourselves
>
> here, now
> this particle of time
> is enough
> to isolate
> to know
> to love

III

Yet, driving the darkness before us
far from limp lettuce, indifferent wine,
although in distant gardens
pink and orange tulips clash,
we envy the illusory purpose of trains
and long to arrange, once and for all,
our lives like unfading watercolours.

BEFORE THE PORTRAIT OF LUCREZIA PANCIATICHI

Lucrezia, grand on the drawing-room wall,
reflecting your green transparent eyes
I braid up bead-roped hair,
compose my brows into swans.
We smooth our pride's four-hundred-year-old lace.

No painter can part these small tight lips.
Crimson shoulders bunched in satin sleeves,
we stiffen from the darkness' warmth
and let long fingers barely touch
the dove-tailed arms of polished wood,
the lustrous, heavy folds.
A little red book in our lap deflects
light from the wedding band's black stone.
Tiny gold letters circle our neck:
Amore — a word we no longer know.

This massive filigreed frame
transfixes our silence like pearls.
We look through illusion,
permit time's brush its stroke
— our long fine nails rigid and sharp.

ACROSS THE PIAZZA

Across the piazza
this Perrier and matchbook afternoon,
I watch the girl in blue and gold stripes
stream down the marble stairs,
uncathedralled hair long-summer light
as doves that sweep
wide rivers of air
from dome to arch
to the cigarette laid ready
beside a glove.

Beyond my glass, the square spreads white with sun
while figures cross
like footed organ pipes,
silent, distanced in their busyness,
as sure, as I am not,
of where the corniced shadows lead,
of what the ancient campanile sings.

My long gaze arcs to catch her blue and gold
flashing haste away on rivered hair.
I want to cup her light
within these shadows,
strike fire
from this blazing afternoon
where my glove,
so cool, so white,
crumples on the café table.

PERDIKA

Back to back with stillness,
hunched in the dimming boulder's curve,
Yani twirls, untwirls a wisp of grass,
carved, like the rock-strewn point, in thought.

His black nanny goat tugs at her tether.
Eyes hard as the halter's ring,
she stiffens splayed knees,
tosses a spiral horn toward water
lapping distant and long
as Yani's fingers spin, spin the wisp warm.
Her black curl of a beard
bobs among purpling flowers,
bleats shaggy hunger, unheard.

Water laps.
Rose stucco houses squat round a blurring shore.
Far away as the fading hills,
mother's dark voice: unbutton, wash hands,
sit to *phasólia* on wooden boards.

Startled, grass twirled in small fingers
opens and flutters down into calm.
Yani tugs thoughts out of stillness.
Stars and nanny goat jostle him home.

MY PRUSSIAN PAST HOLDS NO COMFORT

My Prussian past holds no comfort.
This cobbled street overhung with windows
blinkers the eye, then thins
desire to twin blue spires,
or narrows the other way
to the town's far edge
and a black tree.

Even snug courtyards, arch upon arch
opening ancient and slow
down vined walks to a distant bridge
curving over thick-timbered river,
offer no comfort, although
round calm reminds:
spaces wait to be filled.

Were my rooted forebears happier?
Did climbing tiered vineyards to town
sky eyes with anticipation
for a house to loom round a corner,
a gargoyled door
to glide open?

At night, golden with lamplight and snifters,
leaning back, did they sip and sink
under darkness' unbroken music?
Or strolling arm in arm Sundays
through handkerchief-tidy parks
did they understand
how to uncrinkle pain,
how to nudge the crooked
and set it square?

Stone, high ceilings, night silence
upheld order, walled back
undergrowth creeping the town's far edge.
Behind teacups, my ancestors
balanced politeness and longing,
smoothed troubled hearts like silk sleeves.

That is why I take no comfort in them.

SEA DEEP, AT ST. KITTS

When a man is full, he has no need to dip
under this turquoise-deep and silent rock,
or ponder impossibilities bent down
the rippled moon's green glowing.

Fingers lapped, content, no coral's lace
tears at his hungry touch, dissolves to dark
the solid certainties that lump the shore.
With sunlight, his eyelids warm.

When a man has no midnight drift
pulling his little boat still further out,
when questions come boxed, with lids,
answers tied in yellow bows,

he forgets, if he ever knew, this taut expanse,
untimed solitude that dizzies and pulls
eyes, hands, deeper through luminescent
fish-flit, fern-twirl, long shadows breathing
under the turquoise rock, the rock that sings.

PERSIMMON
For Donia Clenman

From ebony, persimmon flames.
Lush orange flesh, caped in brown-green leaves,
crosses mountains, sand and ocean
to market, among snow apples, maple syrup,
exotic in the corner I.G.A.

Halved in a winter-dark kitchen,
it glows from the wooden cutting board
more brilliant than a Chinese poppy
blazing against the stars.
Between lips, cool pulp quivers,
silk, nectar throbbing the tongue
far off to hanging gardens, swollen bees,
frankincense and ancient stones.

Persimmon:
snow melts
from a white winter plate
as east dawns.

SUDDEN ABSENCE

The week loses all shape,
like a shopping bag bulging sweaters.

You have airplaned the sun south and west,
filling a blue postcard sky
white with sailboats, shirtsleeves and smiles,
undulant hills, your dream realized . . . while I

watch the grey hole where once the sun hung
and shiver beneath layered wool,
clutching limp handles and waiting
for laughter, for light to return.

DUSK, HIGHWAY SEVENTEEN

Your image floats in darkened glass,
ghost across a blur of rock and pine.
Dusk, and the highway jostles you, awake
while overcoats and sweaters doze,
pages rustle and across the aisle
salami crackles from a paper bag.

North. No stars for you, no boreal flash.
Twilight only. Bumpy greyhound dreams
knock the razor edge off loneliness:
you jolt between a hug's confining warmth
and shock of rugged spaces to be crossed.
Alone in your deep shadows strike no light
more constant than a glowing cigarette,
but stare through dust-streaked glass,
ghost, black rock and pine,
and watch time run, and your sharp courage blur.

FAST   SLOW   FAST

Above dark water,
terrace to terrace behind the Summerlea Inn,
tree lights wink toward the Gazebo Bar.
"Two doubles, George!"   "More Heineken."
Glasses clink. Moon-white umbrellas bob.
Rising quadraphonic from hedges,
"Life-in-the-fast-lane . . . " harmonies
float irridescent over the turquoise pool.

Meanwhile in 10:00 p.m. Sewdley
AL'S AIR CONDITIONED
RESTAURANT AND DINING ROOM pounds
"Go, Johnny, Go!" from the upright pianer.
Calluses drum arborite tables 'n chrome.
Plaid sleeves roll up, mop off th' sweat.
"Who had the Special?"   "Golden's on draft."
Orange 'n red thru 40-watt smoke,
linoleum slants warped walls out the door.
Across the dirt road,
on beer cans and rocks
seagulls doze
while slow lake waters lap, lap.

Somewhere between,
we drive down the night,
bug of a car whirring cricket-thick highways.
A billion stars prickle the black.
Tiny, anonymous, lost, we flee
selves cast off far behind like old coats.
Our fear, a doe trying to cross,
freezes in the oncoming beams.

A DOUBLE HOOK

Pale as midnight fish
whipping fins against taut line,
I reel my longings in.

Nothing else waits here,
no ancient wall to slow the water's slap,
no net to catch the moon sinking.
Blackened clouds unroll toward the sea.

What star could prick this night?
Shadows move the wind from weed to pier,
while memories rim the dark,
their low throbbing, a distant highway
followed without a map.

Unseen, I stand,
untangle my emptied line.
There is peace in this lightless moment
spreading between imponderable shores.

BOARDWALK, EARLY MORNING

Walking through heavy fog
we see no forward
no back
only now, here
immobilized in a white dream.

Edges melt
regret fades
a lost green bird
singing from an invisible branch.

Within this opaque mirror
we bump into pieces of ourselves
     startled pink
     stuffed blue
     loom into, out of focus.
Two boards ahead guide our feet.
Fog whites out all cracks beyond.

Blanketed in the unknown
we breathe deep
here, now
freed from shaping a future
and marvel to find our own fingers.

Is this the amazed contentment of ghosts?

PART II
THE BLACK SPECK

PERFECT CANVAS

On this blue and white canvas, the black speck
in the bottom left-hand corner is death.
It doesn't frighten
or spoil the horizontal design:
sand, sea, smooth as unclouded sky.

Instead of a seagull,
it simply is
a flattened fruit fly or bit of grit,
perhaps a flick from the painter's pen
signing another contract to hang
— the unexpected, perfecting dot of an *i*.

For the living
death is a huge black hole
swallowing time, love.
This speck, for the canvas,
strategic dark accent
balancing mass against line.

Ah, the power of art
to contain, to transcend
what we suffer . . . .

DOMESTIC ARTISTRY
For Merla McMurray

As naturally as breath,
her world is arranged.
The little black table, just so, by the kitchen window
quietly knows its place.
Above, geraniums spatter red
counterpoint to the tasteful restraint
of brass agleam from the ceiling rail.
The butcher block demands the centre,
while *Classical French Cuisine* lolls open,
"*Fines Herbes*" addressing tonight's *beaujolais nouveau*.
Even hand-quilted oven mitts
congratulate each other.
The impractical white floor shines.

In this room, as in all the rest,
one never simply is, but glides with grace.

Silent as primitives bordering stucco walls,
tinted pink through cranberry glass,
silvered from napkin rings,
pleasure is $^9/_{10}$ths consciousness:
watching for a nod, that soundless "ah!",
the respect, jealous yet genuine,
for artistry's delicate clasp on life.

IF AGE . . . .
For Franz Wieser

Franz, far out across the bay you float
blue as serenity, yesterday's
paper unlapped in sleep,
brow a smooth pink sun in late afternoon.

Drift free into the opening waves.
Between long trees the house waits,
windows generous, shadows
banished by air and light.

Brown as this flowered wing chair
I sip old Scotch from crystal, dip
behind my eyes, the lake,
and feel the white, massive fireplace,
high oak beams,
the sweeping baronial stair
hold up my love of gracious things.
Skylights open me to the sky.
Space lifts apart walls.
Carpets are quietude.
The music of silence dances between birds.

Dreams: yours water, mine this house,
real as our years return us to ourselves,
plant the stillness of trees.
If age has any virtue
it is this.

KATHLEEN MARSHALL

Widen the window, Kathleen.
With love's long, slow hum
come stalk the flowerbeds,
faded forget-me-not among yellows, reds
bobbing over the sunken sill
tangled with wet-earth scents.

Leave regret to its lost dreams:
trains rushing the high black trestle, from town
plunging into the blue-banked clouds
toward New York, Geneva, Rome.

You were easy in that light:
chandeliers, silver, crystal,
white linen stiff beneath Mozart and wine.
You moved among leather-bound books,
nudes leaning flesh from long gilded walls
until age tore them down.

Come to the flowerbeds,
pull old roots from cedar-thick shadows
wrapping the morning's stillness — the sun
burns through the deepest windows.
Tulips remember only tomorrow.
The grass, though worn, is warm.
A simpler music, this garden,
but enough, enough — hum!

CONVALESCENT

"My last hill remembered,
I look at the quiet carnations,
fresh, white as this gleaming breakfast table.

Lighter than yellowed leaves on the wind,
long I had climbed, through thick grass.
Behind me the locked white rooms,
nightgowns cold with sweat,
I felt a smooth dappled froglet
spring from the wide, flat stones,
rush me high into joy, and smash
against the leaning cliffs of longing.
Plunging breathless we broke on the water,
splashing too dizzy to waggle
sideways to the edge of calm.

Now silence glows in this space between flowers,
the pull of trees leafing
the empty whiteness of plates.
Orange juice is my sun in a little glass,
the blue napkin's silver ring
a piston that moves the sky to spread
across my lazy horizon's lap.

I shall smoke a cigarette,
sift hard pebbles from sand at the river's bend.
I accept my limitations,
water, memory, trees,
kerchunk to none but lost children
— firm as a white coffee mug,
cling to simplicities."

EILEEN AND JEAN

"Today we want to dance
six wrinkled years away,
twist the radio
loud with our living,
tangle our tinted hair,
unbutton down to the rug,
kick caution across the picket fence
neighbours sniff over
watering their own weeds.

Cancer ate my Jack.
Alzheimer's wasted Jean's
— she used to smile from Eatons,
polishing filigreed silver,
ringing up bills like chimes,
wrapping politeness in tissue
softer than *Blue Grass*.
She misses that thread
into brightness, you know.

Me? Fluorescent lights?
Typewriters out-tapping clocks?
I dreamed my daffodilled lawn,
paper Romances, long walks
down to the beach for tea,
sighed my solitude, slow.

Two girls a-blush at men,
we've kept our hemlines straight,
powdered the shine from our loss;
six years, folded our hands,
nodded, patient and neat,
the Meek . . . .

"But today we have to dance!"

IN YOUR LIGHT
For Grandmother Wright

Without frame or lens
to freeze this pine-narrowed bay,
you are clear to me still as shallows
glassing over ridged sand
— the acid clarity of northern rains.

Years have rippled your skin.
Hands like rugged mounts
fist through fishless water,
thrusting cedar and spruce against
sky's low, inverted bowl.

Eyes almost transparent,
you root along this rock.   Through evergreen shade
twisted feet scramble the slope,
shore to stairway, step to shore,
refilling an emptied pail.

When you ease into the boathouse chair,
pink and mauve pansies
bob under white eaves.
Sunned into morning,
your chocolate home sways above water
— with love.

A finger begins
curling, uncurling,
a single strand of white hair.
Memory's mainspring unwinds
clear as the north's thin light.

It was all forest, then,
clustered thick to the sand,
trees chopped down, one by one,
another rock for the pilings dragged up.
A few feet further each year
the fiddlehead tangle flattened,
while lawn spread up the slope,
a slow tide, till it stopped
high enough for four children to run.

Winters back in the city
curled seven days' work round a week:
all your kids helped with the store.
The Great Depression? Contentment:
hot food and enough hand-me-downs.

You married for love and it stuck
fast, on this rock
above skyless water,
building three more
small chocolate houses.
Petunias straightened the lawn.

Cold as the sand
you found him one morning.
Forty-nine years . . . . And now?

You still summer here on your own.
Water curls, uncurls at your door.
Your granddaughter weeds
her begonias.
Others come by
and go.
You can't walk far, but your eyes
absorb the transparent sky.

There are islands
far down the narrowing bay,
little fists punching up
rock, firs reaching
into the wind.

That's the way things are, and stay,
in your light.

WAVES
For Elizabeth Minton

Cold as morning sand
waves' long white tongues
slide beneath your chair,
then froth, run out,
arise, return.

Relentless patience, they pull and push.
A deeper centre impels.
Forward, back,
they mount, lace, spill,
withdraw again to shifting pools.

Rising slowly with wind's cry,
wide they surge, soon horizontal cliffs.
Crests tatter, rage, hiss
blue-black spray from sudden clouds.

Sky falls dark. Cold fury
smashes against your legs.
Possessed, cling to His rock
lost wings batter — or break.

OLD BLACK CAT
For Rappa

At seven in the morning
the old black cat
creeps behind the neighbours' front bushes,
folds into her shadowed, quiet place.
Damp red bricks and ground
hold her safe,
curled from heat, from light.
One yellowed eye watches . . . .

A young tom quivers on the lawn,
white and black
muscled tight to spring
high as birch leaves twittering sparrows,
wide as a shaken, emptied branch.

The old cat yawns.
Beneath that tree she sees him crouch
hungrier each day,
as if birds drop into a waiting mouth.
Stalking — paws' slow motion,
body tunnelling grass —
that's the way to hunt,
but flatfoot there just sits,
or flings himself, flailing,
and down a soft tail feather drifts
untasted.

She had her fill of birds.
Once, even dreams fluttered,
hopped on tiny cat-grumblings.

Now she lies cool,
thinned fur
tufting arthritic bone.

Stalking her,
death is not vicious,
only slow.
Tunnelling wet grass,
it folds her into darkness.
Each day's milk, she laps less and less,
at last just sips from puddled rain.

A redwing titters.
Ears prick up.
Young tom quivers,
tight beneath the tree.

The old cat's eye closes into dream.
One last time,
heart flailing,
can she fling her worn body,
and feather into sky?

SMALL COMFORTS

1. Sleeping With Sylvester

Feathers litter my dream.
Rolling over, I nudge him.

Uncurled from the pink blanket
rumpling my bed,
black fur stretches, long, lean,
tufts a white tummy outward
and purrs.

Robin? Cardinal?
He doesn't care.
Anything round, small, with a beak
— up he flies,
branches, sky flapping paws.
The leap he loves, not the catch.
Panting, he can let go of loss
and just sprawl.

I should learn from him
how to purr,
not snuggle under regrets,
but dart out of cover
after a fresh pair of wings . . . .

Warmed by slow stroking,
closer he wriggles,
flattens along my thigh.
Eyes' green slits sink heavy with sleep.
Big white paws flop, limp.
Pink dreams thicken
and fangs pull back
half-opened into a smile.

I too must breathe soft, deep,
let darkness drift toward dawn.

Black and white fur,
rumpled pink blanket,
we stalk the same golden bird.

2. Chopin & Shadows

After supper, twilight softens the kitchen.
Day's greying edges set straight,
I unknot my apron,
pad to the basement stairs.
Below, hunched at the high black piano,
Grace rehearses Chopin.

I squat on the top step,
next to the cat's darkened bowl,
letting my thoughts run away with the music.
1-2-3, 1-2-3, dizzy *allegros*
lift away wall after wall, until sun
bursts, and old fields warble spring . . . .

Mesto: piano chords slow.
Darkness drops along a valley. Birds still.
By an uprooted tree, I see my father
scan black water for a loose branch
to float shining comfort across to me.
Frank? What's in a name
when death washes between words and hearing?
Ashes to ashes, white hand
dug in my pocket, unable to wave
       I miss you,
          eclipsed, immoveable moon . . . .

CRUNCH! chomps Rapunzel beside me,
eyes yellow crescents of greed.
Waddling the shadows between bowl and bed,
what does she care about Chopin, or crossings?
Birds? Fat illusions behind window panes.

Downstairs, Chopin closes up.
Walls dropped back into place
blaze against sharp kitchen light.
I plug the kettle in,
brew us a fresh cup of tea.
Between sips, Grace and I watch
    a full moon rising
        beyond, through black glass.

ELEGY
In Memory of David Anderson, 1970-1987

At sunrise,
who can believe in death
stalking a pink horizon?
High across hills, shadows run,
slide toward the creek.

Here, in a boy's wilderness
waking under the road,
too much life sings.
A finch flickers frost off a wing,
crickets chirrup first light.

Here is no space for endings.
Mists lift, gilding blue rock and reed.
Leaves flutter the creek orange-red.
Everything alters.
Old bends into new.

Silence is relative, also,
squirrelled quick between rustlings,
or canyoned black behind dawn,
echoes not gone, but transformed
into an unknown tongue.

Here nothing ceases. We live
magnified in a great breath
rustling over woodrushes,
skipping under smoothed stones,
humming silver to gold, twig into sky.

This wilderness under a road,
moment by moment changing,
constantly gathers into itself and absorbs
time, shape, a thousand minuscule deaths,
and sings back a fluid permanence

where nothing, ever, is lost
but, passing at dawn, remembered.

BALANCE SHEET DREAM

Working the brain's curve
luminous numbers like minuscule beads
interconnect on invisible wires.
Pairings and groupings form harmonies,
sets on the left, with those on the right or beneath.

Ping a black bead, and a red one vibrates,
matching the distance, minus or plus.
Magic, each column shivers, lights up.
Decimals rise and fall.

Winking these long winding caves,
nothing functions alone.
Indissolubles, *have* and *owe*,
1 or 0, and 0 or 1
blink back and forth
each to the other
to balance the binary bond.

Within such minute computations
what starred universe unfolds?

PART III
DAWN SNOW

DAWN SNOW

To look out over snow, unbroken
early in morning light, blue, pink
as the soft bum-mound high in the blanketed crib,
is to know fragility's strength.
Snuggled deep under sleep,
breath's little rise and fall
rocks us inevitably onward.
A giant clock's invisible gears
slip softly from notch to notch.

Along the shivering wall,
crocuses sleep, yellow points folded to prayers,
apples dream flame from cold seed.
Summer's purples and greens
wait to burst, like the polka-dot bear
leaning against white bars.

This dawn snow opens on wonder:
our love of perfection, our need
to crunch our own marks through the crust.
Imagine the yard a junction of bird tracks and cats,
brown spears scratching up through.
The pink and blue blanket squirms back,
a small yawn stretches out over the lawn.

BAPTISM
For Julia and John Reibetanz

Incense clouds three solemn priests as Christ
ascends the chancel stairs in slow procession.
Motionless, nine elongated saints
shimmer, watchful, high behind the altar.
We kneel, our music hanging on the Word.

The smaller babies now white-shawled in sleep,
plump as an organ pipe your David gurgles.
His hands make ripples in the golden light
and where the rafters meet, his round gaze stops
caught by smoke and shadow play. He blinks.

Why did God spill water in his eye,
thumb his forehead with odd nursery rhymes?
Mama holds him safe from clustered faces,
bump-bump heart too close for making-strange.
Just ahead the *don't-touch* candles flicker.

We rise and David, brighter than beginnings,
bobs amidst his flock toward the rail.
No white dreams for him: new mysteries
wait in wine and wafer, as the saints,
clouded in watchfulness, bend, tickle his nose.

HAIKU

Daybreak . . .
on the window sill
sparrow's muddy claws.

POEM IN FEBRUARY

Gradually days lengthen.
Beside a road, the land's sparse hairs
poke through thinning snow,
ease aside white anonymity.

We almost sense
warmth tingle beneath the crust
and, in a clarity between clouds,
new light that lifts
blue edges from the afternoon
to pink, to a distant
promise of green.

Our own days try to lengthen,
despite our turning
sparse as spoked grass,
stiffness creeping up seasons,
eyes more hung with sleep.
We are counterpoints to growing:
spring pushes up
out of our subtle, slow decay.

Although we shall wither
among repetitions of flowers,
in this bracing wind
thoughts turn sharp, impatient with regret.
Fruit pressed to wine,
we shall dry in the lengthening sun,
crumble in long shadows

— except for love
that seeds new fields in our hair,
sweeps us on hawk's wide wing across the morning,
beyond unravelling fences,
over the sighing trees
and, high above a dusty, winding thread,
opens in us its golden egg of light.

TREASURE HUNT

When rain slows,
poised close to earth as mist,
and sky smears wet-rag clouds,
we go looking.

Hunched over grit
for pebbles to smooth our palm,
small granite
uneven as arrowheads,
sharp, round, we sort and sieve,
move mud and grains
through thickened brown fingers
. . . no gold.

Salmon and white,
the stones we finally pocket,
smoothing creases from crouched pants.
Hills, tree, sky ripple
across other grey-glass pools
as we clump past.

Rubber boots suck along gouges
trucks ground into the land's long curve.
We stomp past overturned oil drums,
climb a low hill, toward town,
looking for blue to open
behind rain's greased rags,
to wring the sky's last drops
beyond the forlornness of puddles,
to open
fistfuls of gold.

McDIARMID WATCHES THE CHILDREN FISHING

Crouched in the underbrush,
years tucked tight against my chest,
I grip the shaggy crest of a balding hill
and dangle my distanced love down
innocence's silver wires
where fins of laughter flap the rushing pool.

Pull me up,
your catch, slow, steady,
clinging to the curved glistening line.
No trout or bass, I
but whiskered catfish
sliding from darker pools
old as patience,
wiser than forgetting.

I suck your little hooks, greedy,
into my wheezing gills,
dive, resurface,
swing wriggling, wet
over the water's edge,
the grass' swaying,
until, lid pressed tight,
you carry my flopping shadows home
and I rise, wizened knees straight,
tall in remembering.

MOTHERING DAYS
For Stefan

These are mothering days:
hollows warmed with hideouts' flattened grass,
buttercups yellowing under a petal-small chin.

Rolled from ourselves, we watch wind puff clouds
faster than swollen sails dissolving in dream
shapes our lilting fingers trace out of blue.

Hollyhock horses graze on the sun,
nod us to bunch muscles, gallop in rhythms
wild as a wish, wide as our streaming tails
up, over the climbing hills.

The river catches us cold,
splashes surrender, shrieks under willows.
Green in their dappled shade, we twirl
— "Rapunzel, let down your hair."

Fingers splayed, we croak, spring,
bump head-high on reality,
tumble back — hot skin, prickled throats
redden with "Ouch!" and laughter.

The cool house beckons stillness and ginger ale.
Straight, motionless, table and chair
welcome us home to dusk's steady, slow ticking,
old toys patient in corners.
The apple seed cupped on the kitchen sill
is a promise we watch, water again each day.

These are mothering years:
minutes folded back, one by one,
night-light's glow, one more drowsy page,
sleep's blanketed kiss, before the bed
grows shorter and disappears into stars.

RUNAWAYS
For Polly

Tail a rippling wave of fur,
Sporty bounds beside our wind-quick shadows.
The stubble cannot catch us, or the fence
wire us behind rough house and silo.

We have tottered onto rusted barnyard hinges,
dived, arm wide, into the hot tall grass,
swum from head-high corn
and, dried on goldenrod and Queen Anne's lace,
blown ourselves as light
as dandelion fluff, to clouds.

Now, far away as salt licks,
as the mailbox leaning down the thistled road,
we are shining toward the river
flooded black, white with slow cows
dreaming us into the leaf-splashed shallows.

Later, we will herd them behind the gate,
later, lock the evening-narrowed lane
and squatting into darkness
strain to hear sharp mews for crusted milk,
low *hum-suck-suck* from stall to stall,
the separator rattling curds from cream.

We will count down black-tipped stars,
trace languid outlines from the trumpet vines,
and happy as slop pails, muck and matted straw,
watch the barn light yellow
night's white cemented stones,
knowing we are wind-quick shadows, waves
not even the moon can catch.

THE LITTLE DANCERS

Across the yellowed lawn,
rustling leaf points to a blur,
hems diaphanous as dreams
sweep aside old watchful trees.
Hair whirls, uncurls October's thinning light.
Elbows spin off gravity.
From billowing sleeves
pink, white
wings explode.

— Motion
sings.

DUSK, EDWARDS GARDENS

Pond poised like dark glass,
one duck, slipping head-smooth under water,
tails up silence.

AFTER THE CUB MEETING

Racing darkness down the hill,
Stefan flaps open to the wind.
Flying shoes
lace black dew with light.
Fists are balls thrown against the moon.

Faster than the pine-treed night
he grounds the giddy flat,
whoops his starry win, then burns
buttons up the hill again.

BATH/BEDDY

Black, the wood stove dances heat
into his orange wings
wrapped in a shiver of knees, toes
drumming like the sea against
the night's ice.

Tented in touch,
he is a flying horse
— motion, the music
his limbs learn —
six, caught in a blanket's dream,
the sudden flesh of love's warmth.

AT THE ONTARIO SCIENCE CENTRE

1. Vibrations

Behind blackened glass,
strung in wire lines, upright and mute,
tight metallic flowerbuds
jiggle when we whistle:
purple,
amber,
luminescent green.

Mimics of our darkest selves'
stubborn urge to pierce
panes invisible as sound,
in skinny unison their quivering lives
roll
toward my lullabies,
jerk
from stamp and clap,
undulate
right back our need
to hear an otherness.

Startled by their silent waves,
we hone three black reflections
to one, long, glittering thread
— awe.

2. Holograms

Out of darkness, a lion gilds the air.
Slowly we reach to stroke its snout.
Our hands dissolve to gold.

Hovering between dimension and illusion,
the lion devours us, as our eyes consume him.
We stare through streaked mane.
Reality's other side?

Another frame, another lasered film
redden lobster, shimmering conch
where goldfish fin a glass-thick tank
— or are their ripples
photographic traces too?

Ghosts.
The 20th century
burns new light into our brains.

SOLSTICE

Days leaned into low cloud
heavy with the want of snow.
I hung between last leaf and vacant branch,
could not move my blood to love
or hold old shadows' warmth.

Wasted as the wind
I snagged at corners,
waited for the tilting world to turn.

Tonight against my darkened room
the window grows white roofs.
Flakes melt into glass.
Wet, thick silence settles
slow and cold as calm.

FIRST SNOW
For Larry

Winter, like age, tilts our perspective.

The nights take longer.
We wait, with windows less open
pile up the eiderdown.

Padding down a dark hall toward midnight,
we wonder over curled comfort, our children
asleep, while any moment the night-light may shatter,
a canyon open under the dreaming house.

Morning wakens us face-first,
ices feet to the floor.
Defined by the shivering room,
we are separate from snow
banking blue windows,
safe a little while longer
from icicle spears.
Robed in shadows' white breath,
our expectations grow smaller.
We bend, grateful for light, warmth.

In winter we shed delusions,
turn wise:
the universe is a vast and comfortless space,
and we mere specks in its eye.

THE WHEEL

The year is a great wheel.
At the top we ride
rocking-horse ornaments,
tiny red sleighs and stars
moon-high over the frost unafraid.

Poised on a poinsettia point,
our spirits twinkle. Why frown?
Love we sniff in flaming brandy,
joy tastes eggnog-thick on the tongue.
Lungs ring full with carols,
later hush into lullabies.

We have climbed so far
through winter's long nights,
scratched down icicles with bare nails,
skidded through sleet, bone-cracking cold
for one eve to be
merry as children's candle flames
tripping across a frozen window.
We have gathered ourselves
together with ribbons and gifts,
and kissed in hope older than mistletoe.

We have no higher to go
on this wheel that turns
slowly, toward morning
washing red and green faces
white with new-fallen snow.